FLECK

FLECK
by Alasdair Gray

a Comedy in Verse Derived from Goethe's Tragedy of Faust

TWO RAVENS PRESS 2008

Published by Two Ravens Press Ltd
Green Willow Croft
Rhiroy
Lochbroom
Ullapool
Ross-shire IV23 2SF

www.tworavenspress.com

ISBN: 978-1-906120-37-5

British Library Cataloguing in Publication Data: a CIP
record for this book can be obtained
from the British Library.

Book and cover design by Alasdair Gray.
Typeset in Zapf Humanist by Two Ravens Press.

Printed on Forest Stewardship
Council-accredited paper by
Biddles Ltd., King's Lynn, Norfolk.

Mixed Sources
Product group from well-managed
forests, controlled sources and
recycled wood or fiber
www.fsc.org Cert no. TT-COC-002303
© 1996 Forest Stewardship Council
FSC

EDWIN MORGAN
TOM LEONARD
LIZ LOCHHEAD

You, me, everyone we know
          are voices in a conversation
overflowing the edge
               of our wee Scots nation
making England and Germany no bigger,
          nor America nor China too,
for truths are universal and
          three tellers of big truths are **you**.

CONTENTS

CAST LIST

Raphael, Gabriel, Michael: angels who
                 sing or chant in Prologue and Epilogue
Nick: a cosmopolitan almost always on stage
God: a voice with a local accent in Prologue and
        Epilogue, and brief stage appearance in Act 3
Fleck: a great scientist   Acts 1, 2, 3
Earth Spirit: giant face projected on backdrop Act 1
May: a sweet, demure, petite heroine   Acts 1, 2, 3
Martha: older, plumper friend of May   Act 1 & 2
Bill and Jill: university students   Act 1
Two beauticians and a hairdresser   Act 1
Loudspeaker: a voice   Act 2
Waiter: who serves right drinks before asked Acts 2 & 3
MacDuff: a procurator fiscal   Act 2
Jock: a young Glasgow drug dealer   " "
Toady: his cockney henchman   " "
Honey: his moll   " "
Smellie: councillor and online entrepreneur   " "
Lee: Chinese Head of the Global Employers'
                    Federation Acts 2 & 3
Kodak: Lee's American henchman   Acts 2 & 3
Kay: a glamorous press woman   Act 3
Pee: a gutter press man   " "
Cue: a Liberal press man   " "
Television Presenter   " "

PROLOGUE AT
HEAVEN'S GATE

SOUND: *Grand organ chords of religious music in the style of Bach or Handel.*

LIGHT: *A rich dark blue drop curtain rises at back to show a dawn sky with huge crimson sun also rising, slower than the curtain, while changing through orange and gold to white.*

THREE ANGELS in robes coloured like the curtain stand before the sun and chant –

RAPHAEL: The sun-star, glorious as ever,
   bathes all his worlds in golden light
  still rolling round the galaxy
   midst nebulae as vast and bright.
  Planets and moons attend his glory,
   reflect his beams in sparkling ray
  while angels, heralding this story,
   announce the dawning of a day.

GABRIEL: Swift, unimaginably swift
   the mighty earth is rolling too
  from darkness of profoundest night
   to skies celestially blue,
  while winds contest with ocean waves
   or drive them on like fleeing crowds
  against the base of granite cliffs
   whose summits penetrate the clouds –

MICHAEL: Storm clouds, whose snow and hail and rains
   in stream and cataract pour down
  to flood and irrigate the plains
   ensuring growth is nature's crown –
  that seeds take root and creatures feed
   from humble worm to beast of prey,
  while angels, heralding the Lord,
   announce the dawning of his day.

LIGHT: *The sun has disappeared upward, leaving the sky clear blue.*
NICK has approached jauntily through the audience wearing black jeans and scarlet sweater. He mounts the stage as the angels look upward, raising their arms.

LIGHT: *a spot shines down on them.*
ANGELS raise their arms, looking upward to the light while reciting the final verse in unison as NICK bends knees in servile caricature of a courtly bow, raising an arm to the source of light in mocking imitation of the angels.

THE ANGELS: And sounding colour glows and leaps
    twixt star and sun and world and moon –
God is the harmony that keeps
    all nature's orchestra in tune!

LIGHT: *the spot swings out onto NICK.*
NICK jumps up, standing to attention and giving a Nazi salute before speaking with the bonhomie of an experienced gate-crasher.
NICK: Good Lord, it's wonderful to have you here,
and – God Almighty – since you condescend
to let me supervise this bad wee globe,
I'm bound to greet you as a long-lost friend,
my oldest chum. Excuse my slang these days
but since expulsion from your heavenly choir
I've never seen one thing deserving praise
in jargon your angelic mobs admire.
Creation is perhaps a giant joke
that pleases you. Not me! I deal with folk –
men – women – shit, in short. Why give these clods
intelligence? A gift that damned immortal Gods
like me – your deputy! Men would be less bad
without the sciences that make them glad
to torture, kill themselves, their planet too.
GOD has the local accent of a working-class man who, through a university education, has an important professional job. In Scots productions

it should be Scots, and in England any accent
except Oxbridge.

GOD: Do you like nothing here?

NICK: Nothing. The whole mess gars me grew.

GOD: Do you know Fleck?

NICK: Professor Fleck? O yes.
A muddled soul. I laugh at his distress.
A mammy's boy. A teacher's pet. A swot
who hoped the girls would find him fascinating
for knowing what the other lads did not.
That did not fetch them. Missing youthful pleasures
he groped in books for intellectual treasures
till, master of three sciences or four,
he finds professoring a deadly bore
and knows his over-stimulated brain
has done no good, and left him half insane.

GOD: Fleck is unhappy like all honest folk
who do not think the world a giant joke
and find the prize they worked for, hard and long,
is worthless, and has put them in the wrong.

NICK: Aye aye! These very intellectual pains
come easily to men who have no weans
and wives to feed, and do not hear the pleas
of homeless millions, dying of disease.

GOD: Fleck is bewildered. Science and art are born
by those whose inner selves are almost torn
apart by pains that will not let them rest
until they reach the highest and the best.

NICK: Reach you, in fact! How lovely! What if I
prevent that? How about it? Let me try!

GOD: You tried before.

NICK: *[in Yankee]*   – in three-six-nine BC
with Job, your servant? Yep, he sure fooled me.
I knocked his house down, killed his children quick,

stole all his money, left him poor and sick,
his skin one itching scab from head to toe,
then friends arrive, appalled to see such woe,
and to console him, busily explain
he must be wicked to deserve such pain!
Despite the evil things you let me do
that poor sap Job never lost faith in you!
GOD: People with nothing else have only me.
NICK: The **wealthy** are my business? I agree.
Professor Fleck owns nothing rich and fine.
I'll give him all he wants, to make him mine
– if you allow me?
GOD: Do your wicked best.
NICK: Indeed I will! Good Lord I am impressed
by your permissiveness. Moses talked rot
when parroting his slogan, *Thou Shalt Not.*
God forbids nothing. Why do folk forget
the first word that you ever spoke was *Let* –
Let There Be Light! Let there be Lucifer,
and the pervading brightness lets all see
the brightest of your eldest sons is me.
GOD: A fool.
NICK: – who's licensed by your Holiness,
the jester of the universe, no less!
Forgive my levity. I must feel gay
since you are letting me make Fleck my prey.
GOD: Demons like you, Old Nick, I tolerate
because your antics undo something worse –
those smooth routines upholding every state
where management makes government a curse.
Fleck keeps rich managements in good repair.
His well-attended academic courses
turn youths into exploitable resources.
Remove him from his academic chair!

NICK: Dead or alive?
GOD: Alive.
NICK: *[Australian]*   Good on you, God!
        I hate tormenting ghosts. It's much more nice
        to toy with living souls, like pussy toys with mice.
LIGHT: *GOD's spotlight swings back from NICK to*
        his ANGELS.
GOD: My better children, come back to the sky
        and there enjoy the better things we do.
        Make life the loveliest form of energy
        that every day creates the world anew!
SOUND: *Great Amen chords.*
        Curtain closes, leaving NICK on stage facing the
        audience to whom he familiarly remarks –
NICK: I like to see the old dear dropping in
        when weary of his land of endless light
        that gave me heatstroke once. He needs Old Nick,
        and toffs like him are **never** impolite.
        Exit NICK.

— ACT 1 —
FLECK'S STUDY

Backstage   *A wide window so high we cannot see the top.*
  centre: *Outside a starry night sky diagonally crossed by*
            the milky way.
Back left: *A laboratory bench with upon it: a Bunsen*
            burner with low flame under a retort of glowing
            liquid bubbling out along glass tubes; a plastic
            globe of the modern world lit from inside, six
            empty beakers and stoppered vials of liquids.

Back right: *A tall church lectern with brass eagle facing audience, supporting on its wings a great shut book.*

Front left: *A swivel chair at an office desk with computer, slanted to show on the screen a mathematical diagram with lines in several colours.*

Front right: *A narrow spotlight shines on a throne-like armchair.*

LIGHT: *low enough on stage to show up bright bench apparatus and computer screen. There is a spot on the armchair.*
FLECK, bearded, looking stout in a quilted dressing gown, sits in armchair holding a skull over which he broods morosely.

SOUND: *Westminster chimes strike the half hour.*

FLECK: Psychology – I mastered that,
biology and physics too.
In each I've made discoveries
my colleagues lecture on as true, the fools.
[stands and wanders uneasily about]
One certainty my knowledge brings –
science and wisdom are quite different things.
Why call my colleagues fools? I'm just as bad.
[puts skull down on desk or bench]
Students pour in to pay their fees,
swallow my words and use my knowledge
to stay behind and teach in college
or start their own consultancies.
Who once had gained high office in the Church
are now engaged in highly-paid research.
I once believed the sciences I taught
were founding universal brotherhood.
Psychologists today become spin doctors,

Biologists are making cheap, fast food.
The physicists invent new ways of killing
for sale to terrorists of every nation –
government forces or their enemies –
both sides enrich a global corporation.
I can't go on like this. I have to change,
how? I must call on what, to me, is strange –
occultism. Self-hypnosis. Artful tricks
which once got people burned as heretics.
No wonder! *[he goes to lectern]*
                    Nostradamus wrote this book.
[he opens it]
LIGHT: *Blue glow from the book shines on his face.*
He knew some things smart moderns overlook.
These starry signs can give a man control
of forces that still shape the human soul.
LIGHT: *As he turns pages more colours light his face.*
Dealings with Mercury would make me rich,
or Bacchus elevate me with his wine.
Venus could turn me into a Don Juan,
Apollo make my singing voice divine.
Mars, giving victory through martial art,
might make of me another Bonaparte.
Great Jupiter has made more lasting kings,
but heads of state today are feeble things.
Such partial gods divide the human soul —
where is the spirit that can make it whole?
LIGHT: *a page lights his face more strongly.*
The sign of the Earth Spirit! – yes, the Earth
alone can give a man his second birth.
[He gazes in wonder.]
I think that I begin to understand it
but do I have the courage to command it?
No solid mass of mineral density

but a great fountain of vitality
or else a strongly rooted wind-tossed tree
with many gleaming fruits among the leaves –
fruits that are living souls. And is one me?
[With violence.]
No! I am God's image – shaped from earthly clay
but with a soul that never shall decay!
Anything less than God must be my brother.
[Rips out page, holds it up, staring at it.]
Earth Spirit, visit me in human form
for you and me must talk to one another!

SOUND: *a tremendous musical chord with fading echo.*

The night sky beyond window is replaced by a dazzling face so big that at first only an eye, then mouth, are completely visible. FLECK drops the page which a gust sweeps into the wings. The SPIRIT's voice is clear, with slight echo.

SPIRIT: Why do you call?

FLECK, with inarticulate cry, reels, shuddering.

SPIRIT: Answer! Why call me here?

FLECK clutches his hair.

SPIRIT: Why do you call me? Answer! Are you dumb?

FLECK: Go! … Back! … A little further back! My fear …
is almost overcome.

The SPIRIT recedes so that the face fills the doorway, the face of a pre-adolescent child, indignant yet mocking.

SPIRIT: Fear almost overcome?
Where is the insolence that called me brother
and tried to give itself a better goal
by forcing me into this tête-à-tête,
to recreate your wretched little soul?

FLECK: You daunted me at first, great spirit, true.
Not now! Now I command you to renew
the thing I am by saying what you are!

SPIRIT: I am the only planet of your star
to carry living souls who question me.
In calms and storms and foaming waves
I bring new forms from birth to graves,
steadily blending, coming and going,
brief but unending lives overflowing,
from ocean depths up to the windswept sky
I weave for God the clothes you see Him by.
Hearing this, FLECK has grown confident.

FLECK: O noble spirit, working through time and space
to make this sordid globe a better place,
thank you! A thousand thanks for now I see
we are alike!
The SPIRIT speaks through silent laughter.

SPIRIT: You see what you're imagining! – Not me!

FLECK: *[yells]* Not you?

SOUND: *Tremendous musical chord as face dwindles to
vanishing point in night sky.*

FLECK: I made that ... thing appear before my eyes
and questioned it, and listened to replies,
and glimpsed a being similar to mine
sharing a purpose that I thought divine,
yet saw it falsely! Why do I exist?
Professor Fleck's a paltry solipsist!
An academic fraud! Impotent too!
Useless and sexless –

SOUND: *loud knocking.*

FLECK: *[in a snarling shout]* Who the hell are you?
*Enter NICK as an enthusiastic spectacled lad
with tousled hair, wearing slippers and pyjamas
under an open white laboratory coat, a half*

bottle of whisky in the pocket.
The audience need not at once notice he
is NICK. FLECK, disgusted, slumps down in
the big chair.

NICK: Excuse me sir, I think you were rehearsing
a tragedy translated from the Greek.
Though just a residential lab assistant
a grasp of languages is what I seek.
A scientist like you I'll never be,
but might become a guru on TV
telling folk what we do in this laboratory,
making it sound like fun, if I'd the oratory.
Tell me sir, would a course of drama teach
a lad like me a better flow of speech?

FLECK: Your present flood of words is adequate –
smooth eloquence is wholly out of date.
Broadcasters think the public is a fool
so sounding stupid is their golden rule.
If you would like to be more widely known
don't try to change your... slightly vulgar tone.

NICK: Wonderful news!
                [thoughtfully] A bit depressing too,
if famous me can never be, like you,
looked up to!

FLECK: You'd be envied for your fame.

NICK: You make that seem a rather pointless game.
I'll think about it. Sorry I barged in.

FLECK: Carter, I'm glad. Your unexpected knocking
prevented me indulging in a shocking
burst of self-pity, I regret to say.

NICK: Yes, many folk feel like that on Hogmanay.

FLECK: Hogmanay?

NICK: Soon we will hear the bells.

FLECK: Year gone and nothing gained. *[groans]*

NICK: My granny tells
me time goes faster as we use years up.
Let's welcome, sir, the new year in a cup
of what the Scots call kindness – raise a cheer
with friends who've come to welcome the new year,
fine girls among them! You need a party, so –
                                    [produces whisky bottle]

SOUND: *Westminster chimes before the stroke of
midnight.*

FLECK: Carter, it's peace I need. Thank you, but go!
[violently]
Please leave. A party? Surely not. No! No!
*NICK leaves with grimace, shrug and sharp
backward glance. FLECK stands and approaches
the bench back left, talking loudly, heavily, slowly,
each of his lines punctuated by a midnight stroke
of the bell.*

FLECK: Carter, that idiot, **(1)** stopped me going mad.
The very greatest, **(2)** fun-da-men-tal cause
of me and all I know **(3)** both good and bad
declared I could not **(4)** see the thing it was.
So! I twist every **(5)** thing to selfishness?
True, but I can't **(6)** continue in this mess.
[he lifts bottle from bench, unstoppers it]
To be, or not? Not! **(7)** I will pour my own
cup of kindness. Mhm **(8)** Phe-no-bar-bi-tone
[pours measure into beaker]
will end my year so **(9)** Fleck, why hesitate?
Courage, Professor! **(10)** Come, embrace your fate.
You don't fear death. **(11)** You don't believe in Hell.
This cup of kindness **(12)** will make all things well.
*FLECK raises the beaker to his lips.
Simultaneously –*

SOUND: *of wild chiming bells, fireworks crackling as rocket explodes in night sky. NICK, in sweater and trousers, pulling MAY by one hand, MARTHA by the other, bursts in with JILL and BILL in fancy dress and paper party hats, singing. BILL with two bottles of wine. FLECK stares, astonished.*

THE PARTY: A guid new year to ane and a'
and mony may ye see!
And here's tae a' the years tae come
and happy may they be!
NICK pulls the two women over to FLECK shouting over the song –

NICK: Because, Professor, you are far far too busy to join the girls, they come to you!
[he grabs and flings away the beaker]
Now then!
The bemused FLECK, his hands seized by MAY and MARTHA, is pulled into a ring of NICK hand-in-hand with MAY and JILL and BILL (who has put his bottles on the floor) hand-in-hand with JILL and MARTHA. They dance sideways singing –

MARTHA: Should auld acquaintance be forgot,
And never brought to mind?

MAY: We'll tak a cup o kindness yet
For auld lang syne.

EVERYONE: For auld lang syne, my jo,
For auld lang syne
We'll tak a cup o kindness yet
For auld lang syne.
The ring dances the opposite way with FLECK starting to be amused.

MAY: We twa hae paidl'd in the burn,
And pu'd the gowans fine,

MARTHA: But seas between us braid he roar'd
                                  Sin' auld lang syne.
EVERYONE: For auld lang syne, my jo,
                                  For auld lang syne
          We'll tak a cup o kindness yet
                                  For auld lang syne.
          All cross hands to shake each other's, narrowing
          the circle.
MAY: Then here's a hand, my trusty fiere!
MARTHA: And gie's a hand o' thine!
MAY AND And we'll tak a right gude-willie waught
MARTHA: For auld lang syne.
          FLECK now looks and laughs from one girl to
          the other who laugh back.
EVERYONE: For auld lang syne, my jo,
                                  For auld lang syne
          We'll tak a cup o kindness yet
                                  For auld lang syne.
          The ring breaks. NICK, without releasing MAY's
          hand, pulls her to the desk and sits on it, pushing
          her down into the swivel chair. MARTHA, older,
          plumper and more sexily dressed, pulls FLECK
          by the hand to his own chair. He collapses into
          it with relief, she sits on the chair arm, snuggling
          against him. BILL lifts the bottle, goes with JILL
          to the bench. He empties the bottle into six
          beakers, then serves NICK and MAY with two
          as JILL takes two to FLECK and MARTHA; then
          JILL and BILL amuse themselves at the bench
          with the other two glasses and the skull, before
          going to the lectern where BILL enjoys turning
          the book's pages to show images JILL pretends
          to find shocking or frightening. Meanwhile the
          others converse, MARTHA talking to FLECK

who answers absentmindedly because he is
looking across at MAY, NICK talking to MAY
who is intrigued by the sight of FLECK and
MARTHA.

FLECK: One of my students are you?

MARTHA: Don't you know?

FLECK: When lecturing my mind's on what I teach.

MARTHA: You don't see faces?

FLECK: No need. The exams show
who listens.

MARTHA: O? You failed me in psychology.
FLECK is amused.

FLECK: I hope you're not expecting an apology.
Both sip from their beakers.

NICK: Behold Professor Fleck learning to flirt!

MAY: He isn't streetwise.

NICK: Worried he'll get hurt?
You like big daddies?

MAY: I don't like you, Carter!

NICK: Of course! I'm a Smart Alec – no-one smarter.
No decent girls want **me** I'm glad to say.
Drink up!

FLECK: *[still watching MAY]* Will you repeat the year?

MARTHA: *[nodding]*   I've paid my fee.

FLECK: Mature student?

MARTHA: Twice divorced. You see –

FLECK: *[interrupts, raising forefinger]*   Please!
Give me no details. I'm no wise confessor
but just your rather immature professor.

MARTHA: *[smiling]* We all know that.

FLECK: *[indifferent]*   Who is this all who know?

MARTHA: Your female students, sir.

FLECK: *[mildly interested]*   How does it show?

MARTHA: Not looking at us straight is the reaction

of someone terrified of our attraction
unless we're out of reach, like my friend May.
FLECK, for once, looks straight at MARTHA.

FLECK: Is that her name? Perhaps you think I'm gay?

MARTHA: *[laughing]* O no sir. You're as miserable as Hell.
FLECK, laughing, raises her hand to his lips and kisses the back of it.

FLECK: I failed you in psychology! Well well!

NICK: *[to MAY]*
Professor Fleck's emerging from his shell.
But Martha's not his type. It's you, my dear,
he'll want when he relaxes – never fear.

MAY: That's stupid! I am no professor's pet.

NICK: Not now you ain't! But he'll surprise you yet.

MAY: He's far too dignified, too old, too stout!

NICK: Inside him there's a young chap wanting out.
NICK empties his glass down his throat, claps hands, leaps to middle of the floor and shouts –

NICK: My friends! My friends!
Bad news! Bad news! Bad news!
It's Hogmanay and we've run out of booze!
Groans from BILL, JILL and MARTHA.

NICK: There's plenty in my room – you know the way!

BILL: Three cheers for Carter! Hip hip hip –

BILL, JILL, MARTHA: Hooray!
MARTHA empties her glass as BILL and JILL leave, and stands, saying to FLECK –

MARTHA: Coming?

FLECK: No.

MARTHA: You ought to come! Cheerio.
MARTHA leaves as NICK pulls MAY across to FLECK.

NICK: Professor, this shy girly wants to say – what is it?

MAY: Thanks.

FLECK: *[rises]* For what? I gave you nothing, May.
You helped to save my life.

NICK: *[laughing]*   He's right! That's true!
*MAY and FLECK gaze into each other's eyes,
then abruptly she runs out. NICK slaps FLECK
on the shoulder and strolls away, highly
pleased with himself, chortling and rubbing
hands. FLECK, arms folded on chest, stands
watching him curiously.*

FLECK: Carter, what are you?

NICK: *[to the audience]* He's rumbled my wheeze.

FLECK: Rumbled?

NICK: I turn to slang at times like these,
being embarrassed by the fact that I
(though your assistant) am a … sort of … spy.

FLECK: Who for? The government?

NICK: *[scratching his head]*   I'll start again.
Forgive me! It's not easy to explain.
*FLECK sits back in his chair, cheek on fist,
prepared to be bored.*

NICK: I am a part of what was endless night
before a greater part discovered light.
That bigger part is everybody's dad –
boss of all things, including you, my lad.
Dad has (don't ask **me** why) conceived a plan
that needs you to become a greater man.

FLECK: I know our universities are now infested
with spies. I am just not interested. *[yawns]*
And everybody's dad? Stop talking rot.
Police chiefs do not think that way.

NICK: Why not?
My brother, who's a simpleton and dunce,
became a carpenter's apprentice once.

               Why should his older brother not be earning
               cash as your lab-boy in this seat of learning?
               I'll tell you why! Working here stunts my growth,
               just as it's stunting yours. It's time we both
               set out for fresher fields and pastures new.

FLECK: Carter, I am alive because of you
               and grateful, but please tell the CIA
               or MI5 or any other boss,
               Fleck's not for hire. They'll find me no great loss.
               NICK raises his eyes to Heaven, punches his
               brow, flings away his spectacles and goes to
               FLECK saying –

NICK: O Fleck Fleck Fleck! Why must you be so thick?
               Look at me! *[grasps Fleck's shoulders]*
                              Can't you see that I'm Old Nick?

FLECK: *[without getting up]* Give me a sign.
               NICK stands back, snaps his fingers.

SOUND: *deafening crash of thunder.*

LIGHT: *instant on-stage darkness with, in window, dark*
               red sky and branched lightning.

SOUND: *another crash of thunder.*

LIGHT: *at once previous night sky and stage lights are*
               resumed.
               FLECK, sitting up in his chair, watches NICK
               who faces him from a distance, hands on hips.

NICK: Are you convinced?

FLECK: A cinematic trick,
               impressive though. And what else can you do?

NICK: Some hocus-pocus stuff transforming you.
               FLECK stands up, alarmed.
               Worry ye not! The change, when I unfold it,
               will please you very much when you behold it.
               [claps his hands]
               Music and cosmeticians come to me!

Make over Fleck as he would like to be!

SOUND: *sinister, sensual music.*

LIGHTS: *grow dimmer except for revolving coloured spots cast by disco ball.*
TWO FEMALE BEAUTICIANS *and HAIRDRESSER skip in with trolley holding tools of their trade. They wear purple clothes that are otherwise conventional. Their ballet with* FLECK *(who is dazed and passive) removes his thickly padded gown, taking away enough bulk to show an athletic figure in black slacks and white shirt. They press him into the chair, drape a barber's sheet round him, turn the chair-back to audience.* HAIRDRESSER *shaves and trims* FLECK *helped by the women who present towels, razors, combs, brushes, moisturisers.* NICK *strolls around, sometimes watching with approval, sometimes slightly bored.* HAIRDRESSER *whisks off sheet, swivels chair round and helps to his feet a handsome new beardless* FLECK *as the* BEAUTICIANS *pull in from the wings a tall mirror on casters, turning it to show* FLECK *his new image.* HAIRDRESSER *and* BEAUTICIANS *skip out with trolley and mirror as –*

SOUND: *music stops,*

LIGHTS: *go normal.*
FLECK *turns to* NICK *who contemplates him smugly.*

FLECK: Why have you done this?

NICK: To display my might.

FLECK: Old Nick's an exhibitionist?

NICK: Not quite.

I am a salesman. This is an example
of goods I'm selling. Call it a free sample.

FLECK: Your other goods?

NICK: Sex, money, power and glory.

FLECK: Paid for in Hell?

NICK: Please disregard that story.
You pay for them in Hell, but never fear.
Your Hell is not eternal. It is here.

FLECK: Hell is on earth?

NICK: On earth – I won't deceive you,
the goods I'm offering will often grieve you.
Self pity for the hearts you have to break –
regret for lives you ruin by mistake –
the loneliness of being rich and great
and hated by all who envy your estate –
are tedious at times. I must confess
self pity and regret and loneliness
are what you'll pay me for the goods I sell.

FLECK: I've known these all my life.

NICK: [cheerfully]   Welcome to Hell!
You'll find the game well worth the entrance price,
but first, a word of warning and advice.
The satisfying of each splendid sense
may place a burden on your conscience
unless you shake it off.

FLECK: Can that be done?

NICK: Of course! With drink and drugs–but it's more fun
to lose old deeds by plunging into new.
Rapid activity's the drug for you.
All passionate delight in womankind
produces babies or a broken heart.
All schemes to make the world a better place
must break some heads and spoil some works of art.
In the destructive element immerse!

　　　　　　I'll teach you swimming, Fleck – it is your fate
　　　　　　to be magnificent! Dare to be great!
　FLECK　You have not told me why you offer this.
　　　　　　After a pause NICK speaks unwillingly.
　NICK:　I do it to annoy someone I hate.
FLECK:　Why does God let you?
　NICK:　*[desperately]*　　　　Please! Forget that shit!
FLECK:　You're hiding something that I need to know.
　　　　　　NICK sighs then says in cockney –
　NICK:　Rumbled my wheeze again, you cunning lad.
　　　　　　[soberly]
　　　　　　The whole thing started many years ago
　　　　　　when there was perfect peace, secure, blank, black,
　　　　　　featureless, timeless, silent cosiness
　　　　　　till someone moved. With a tremendous crack
　　　　　　eternity became a gibbering mess
　　　　　　of substances. The universe **became**!
FLECK:　We call it The Big Bang.
　NICK:　*[snarling]*　　　　Too kind a name!
　　　　　　I call it The Big Fart. The gas condensed
　　　　　　in globes that burst apart, waltzing around
　　　　　　each other while they fled, half blinding me
　　　　　　who loved the kindly night before that first
　　　　　　and worst of movers shattered my warm bed.
　　　　　　The echo of his fart rings in my ears.
　　　　　　FLECK is amused.
FLECK:　It has been called the music of the spheres.
　NICK:　Spectacularly pointless radiation
　　　　　　was not enough for that prolific toff
　　　　　　who spat it, shat it out. He wanted admiration!
FLECK:　But God has angels.
　NICK:　　　　　　　　Aye, a heavenly host
　　　　　　who think he's the bees' knees, but dogs don't boast
　　　　　　of their fleas' appreciation. **Free** love

was what God wished. The one free mind was mine,
I loathed that dog-spelled-backward's whole creation.
"What use are your billion zillion worlds?" I cried.
"What use are new-born babies?" he replied,
teasing me with a wholly senseless word.
A million zillion centuries elapsed
before the first babies occurred.

FLECK: So God foresaw men before life began?

NICK: God knows what God foresaw—I don't, young man.
The babes he looked to maybe were jellyfish,
worms, centipedes, any low form of life
except those pissing, squawking manikins
who grew up to be Adam and his wife.

FLECK: And that was when you came to earth?

NICK: *[sighing]*   O no.
I came here long long long long years ago.
NICK speaks the next nine lines in Cockney.

NICK: One day Almighty Gawd, 'e sez ter me,
"Nicky, let us agree ter disagree.
"'Ere's a young planet – nufink too immense –
"where molecules is shuffling into sense
"and that means life, my boy! So you go there
"and do your best to ruin the affair.
"I'm all for life," sez 'e, "but if you can
"manage to stamp it out, then you're the better man."
"Want a bet, guv?" I sez to 'im, "Alright!"
[speaking as usual]
And that is why I've met you here tonight.

FLECK: But life has triumphed!

NICK: *[shrugging]*   So far, so it seems.

FLECK: What place have I in your destructive schemes?

NICK: His Holiness and I both want to see
how you will use the powers that make you free
to do just what you want.

FLECK: Well, first of all
        I want a good night's sleep.
  NICK: A good idea. Start small. *[snaps fingers]*
LIGHT: *Immediate darkness.*

— ACT 2 —
THE CASINO

A lounge with a big central entrance at the back leading to darker, busier rooms. The lower quarter of this entrance is hidden by the high back of a very long slightly curved luxurious sofa with a table before it at each end. Far left and right are two similar, much shorter sofas, each with a single table in front. Those entering use the left or right gaps between the three sofas.
Enter left NICK and FLECK in evening wear.

LOUD—   Ladies and gentlemen, in ten minutes the
SPEAKER: Grand National will be televised in the Lady
          Godiva Suite where you will be served by
          topless barmaids, so place your bets and
          take your seats!
          NICK settles easily on left sofa, hands
          clasped behind head, left leg over right.
          FLECK stands looking distastefully around.
FLECK: A gambling den.
NICK: Where you're going to meet
          winners and losers who will change your life.
          Drunks squander faster, so the drinks are free,
          financed by what lawyers, bankers, councillors,
          drug dealers lose on a gambling spree.
FLECK: I don't gamble, don't booze.
NICK: Very wise. Nor do I.
          But you have trousered a Nobel Prize, John.
          We must celebrate! Soon May will be here and,
          I tell you straight, May is your fate.
          FLECK frowns, sitting down as WAITER
          approaches with tray set with tea things.
FLECK: Did she drag me to a chair on Hogmanay?
NICK: May is not plump – May is sweet, demure, petite,
          and (forgetting French)
          [in throaty Yankee voice]
                          a damned good lay.
          [in posh English voice]
          Let us share a dish of tay.
          WAITER puts tray on table and withdraws.
          NICK lifts pot.
NICK: Shall I be mother?…A little milk? One lump or two?
LOUD—   Ladies and gentlemen, in ten minutes a
SPEAKER: game of baccarat and nude mud wrestling
          will commence in the Marie Antoinette

Suite. Take your seats.

Enter MACDUFF right, who sits calmly to the right of the back sofa where the WAITER serves him a glass of brandy as JOCK, TOADY and HONEY enter right behind him. This is their first encounter with rich company. JOCK feels uneasy but rebellious. He sits in middle of right sofa, hands clasped between knees. HONEY sits beside him. TOADY, impressed, sits on the other side after saying –

TOADY: Wot an amazin place!

HONEY: You're very quiet, Jock.

JOCK: I am tense.

This pleases TOADY, worries HONEY.

TOADY: Which could lead to a fight! Am I right?

HONEY: Only if he hears a remark he dislikes –

TOADY: *[amused]* He won't hear one from me!

HONEY: Or me –

JOCK: Of course not. Yous are my team, so we agree.

HONEY: Jock, don't start a fight here, the bouncers are tough.

TOADY: Not as tough as Jock's team when the chips
                                              are down!

JOCK: *[brightening]*
And the flag goes up and starting pistol fires!

MACDUFF: Talk more quietly please.

TOADY eagerly, HONEY frightened, stare tensely at JOCK who, after a pause suddenly smiles at MACDUFF as the WAITER approaches them, tray in hand.

JOCK: *[calmly]*   You said please, Mr MacDuff.
I like good manners. Your manners are good enough.
MACDUFF looks away contemptuously as JOCK tells the WAITER –

JOCK: Apple juice for me, big malt for him,

gin and coke for Honey…
WAITER offers them.

JOCK: You knew I drink that?
[throws note onto tray] Here's fifty quid.
Keep the change. I'm not short of money.

LOUD— Ladies and gentlemen, in ten minutes a game
SPEAKER: of blackjack and bare fist cage boxing will
commence in the Emperor Nero Suite. Take
your seats.

FLECK: Is that legal?

NICK: Clubs that pay the police enough
can get a license for almost anything.
[points to MACDUFF before hailing him]
There's our Procurator Fiscal! Hello, MacDuff!

MACDUFF: Why, hello Nick. You turn up everywhere.

NICK: Yes, I'm as busy as you!
*Enter SMELLIE with confident MARTHA on
his arm, shy MAY slightly behind. They go
to sit with MACDUFF watched by JOCK and
his team and NICK but not by FLECK. MAY,
looking at the floor, sees nobody.*

MACDUFF: Councillor Smellie and twa bonnie lassies!
Introduce me.
*WAITER puts tray with champagne bottle
and four glasses on their table.*

SMELLIE: Martha, meet legal eagle Harry MacDuff.
This shrinking violet is Martha's friend, May
who should perk up after some bubbly
that has popped in –
WAITER pops out the champagne cork.
FLECK looks across at the sound.

SMELLIE: – at just the right time of day.
WAITER fills the glasses.

MACDUFF: A glass for me? You're really far too kind!

TOADY: Cor, look at them bints! Just look! I wouldn't mind giving one of them a stiff hard present.

HONEY: Toady! Don't talk unpleasant. I'm a lady too.

TOADY: *[scornfully]* A lady? You?

JOCK: *[fiercely]*   Belt up! Honey's mine so a lady tonight! *[thoughtfully]* But in a way Honey, Toady's right. I wish you dressed like her. *[points]*

HONEY: *[indignant]* Dress like a hoor?

JOCK: The thin one, not the fat. *[wistfully]* I would pay to dress **you** like that.

HONEY: *[sarcastic]* Ta muchly!

JOCK stares at MAY, as FLECK is doing.

NICK: That's her. That's May. Time you two lovebirds met.
He goes to the MACDUFF group. MAY looks up.

MAY: Carter!

MARTHA: Fancy meeting you, Carter!

MACDUFF: But this is –

NICK swiftly interrupts.

NICK: A natural mistake! I'm Carter's older brother. Fancy meeting **you**, Councillor Smellie, our great new sportsman!

SMELLIE: *[protesting but amused]*
                              Why? I hate games, Nick!

NICK: You've bought a football **and** a rugby club! Is that not true?

SMELLIE: *[nodding]* Both clubs now share one pitch.

MACDUFF: Leaving the other pitch for you to sell?

SMELLIE: No. To rent.

MARTHA: To who?

SMELLIE: To me.

NICK: *[laughing]*   Merry hell!

That's truly creative accountancy!
[He tells MAY quietly]
John Fleck over there wants a word with you.
*MAY, surprised and grateful, leaves the sofa
and her champagne glass and goes to FLECK
as NICK sits in her place, lifts her glass and
sips from it, asking SMELLIE –*

NICK: Why pay rent for your own property?

SMELLIE: My Independent Finance Initiative
is going to build a big new school there
for kids whose schools we're closing everywhere.
It will have three internal playgrounds on
first, nineteenth and thirty-seventh floor for
nursery, primary and comprehensive
secondary classes.

MARTHA: You'll pile the kids high?

MACDUFF: The older they get, the nearer the sky!

NICK: A wonderful way to elevate the masses!
*They all laugh while MAY, timid yet eager,
stands gazing at FLECK who gazes hopefully
back.*

MAY: Professor Fleck – O I am glad to see **you**.
This is a strange place. It's my first time here.

FLECK: Please sit down and please call me John.
I'm a beginner here too.
*She sits and they continue gazing at each
other, watched by JOCK, who frowns. Enter
at the left entrance LEE and KODAK who
sit down on the far left of the central sofa
followed by WAITER who serves them with
modest cocktails. They are ignored by JOCK's
team but noticed by those with MACDUFF.*

LOUD— Ladies and gentlemen, take your seats for a
SPEAKER: new game of roulette in the Marquis de Sade

suite where the Torture Theatre will present its new cabaret *Panties Inferno*.

MAY: I don't like this place, John.

FLECK: No. It's vile.
I was about to leave before I saw you.
WAITER puts two cocktails before them and removes tea tray.

FLECK: *[smiling]* Will one drink hurt us?

MAY: *[smiling]*   Perhaps not.
They clink glasses, then sip, FLECK gazing at her face. MAY becomes anxious.

MAY: Is something wrong with my makeup?

FLECK: *[dreamily]* Do you wear any?

MAY: *[smiles, reassured]* You're looking so hard at me!

FLECK: *[smiling]* You have a lovely face.

MAY: *[impulsively]* You have a lovely smile.
MACDUFF, SMELLIE, MARTHA study LEE and KODAK who NICK seems to ignore.

MACDUFF: Our club is getting cosmopolitan.

NICK: In a **big** way.

SMELLIE: What do you mean?

NICK: They're here to rent Dunfermline Business Park for a summit conference on global hygiene.

MARTHA: Who are they?

NICK: The Chink is Chang Lee, chairman of Global Employers' Federation.
The Yank is his sidekick Kodak. Excuse me.
NICK rises and goes over to LEE and KODAK as MARTHA stares, awestruck, and MACDUFF quietly tells SMELLIE, who nods –

MACDUFF: Nick knows bosses in every nation.

KODAK: By G and J Nick! Why are you here?
NICK sits beside LEE, speaks on an intimate note while indicating FLECK with a slight gesture.

NICK: You see him? John Fleck, Lee!
  LEE: *[nodding]*   The Nobel winner?
KODAK: Sorry Nick. That name means nothing to me.
  NICK: No need for apology, Kodak,
        but John Fleck's finding of an interface
        between physics, plant growth and psychology
        are more than substantial – they confirm
        Einstein's unified field equation.
        KODAK shakes his head, grinning.
KODAK: The equations **we** handle are financial.
  LEE: Fleck's equations open new power sources?
  NICK: Cheap ones, in every nation.
KODAK: Then Fleck's discovery has a highly
        revolutionary implication.
  LEE: What are his politics?
  NICK: You are in luck.
        He's a research chemist who can't see far
        past his laboratory table, but
        has found love so you are able to make him
        offers he won't refuse.
KODAK: Mm! I call that real good news.
        NICK stands up saying –
  NICK: Fleck is an essential man —
        take him on board if you can.
        *LEE sits quietly watching FLECK to almost the
        end of the Act, the only man not disturbed
        by what follows. NICK approaches JOCK
        saying pleasantly –*
  NICK: You recognise me, Jock?
  JOCK: *[unsure]*   I … think I do …
  NICK: I am the one who makes your dreams come true.
        From me comes all the ecstasy you sell
        (behind my back of course) to all our clientele.
        [in a low voice]

A big consignment's stashed behind the door
of you-know-where. Mix it up one in four.
The girl your eye is fixed on will be yours
if you approach her in the proper way.

HONEY: But Jock, she's got a man!
NICK: Poo! He's timid, old and gay!
A tiny threat from you will make him run
leaving the wench to you, who's handsome,
                                    brave and fun!

*NICK snaps fingers and WAITER approaches,
three brandy glasses on salver, as JOCK gazes
hungrily at MAY.*

JOCK: Thanks for the tip ... I see that. Yes, I do!
*NICK lifts two glasses, places one in JOCK's hand.
The WAITER stands by.*

NICK: Let's drink to that. Brandy for heroes.
                                    Tickety boo!

*He clinks his glass against JOCK's, flings back
head, swallows brandy in one gulp. JOCK
imitates him, splutters, staggers, quickly
recovers, places empty glass on WAITER's tray,
then stares again at MAY. HONEY puts a hand
on his sleeve.*

HONEY: But Jock!
JOCK: [not looking at her] Who's boss here, bitch?
HONEY: [whispering]   You boss! You!

*NICK hands JOCK the third full brandy glass
and speaks into his ear.*

NICK: Her name is May. Now go in for the kill.
*JOCK, squaring shoulders, crosses the floor to
MAY and FLECK who, gazing into each other's
eyes, don't see him before he speaks.*

JOCK: May, you don't know me yet, but soon you will!
FLECK: Excuse me!

JOCK: Faggot, I like your suit –
[flings brandy onto front of FLECK's trousers]
                  pity about the stain.
Now take it to the cleaners.

FLECK: *[jumping up]*   You're insane!
JOCK shouts to everyone else, pointing to FLECK's trousers.

JOCK: Fling this man out! He's pissed his pants! You see?
The women stare while all men but LEE stand to see what's happening.

FLECK: You drunken idiot!

JOCK: *[growling]* Don't use those words to me!
JOCK produces a flick-knife and lunges.
NICK leaps toward them with a single cry –

NICK: Stop everyone!

SOUND: *abrupt musical chord. At which:*
All but NICK stand frozen.

SOUND: *a droning echo of the chord continues behind the following action:*
NICK points to FLECK saying –

NICK: **You** don't stop! Disarm that fool!
NICK steps back, watching with folded arms. Everyone else stays rigidly frozen as FLECK, after a puzzled pause, slowly extends his right hand toward the fist holding the knife but, before touching it, looks at NICK who smiles and nods encouragingly. FLECK, with an effort, plucks the knife from JOCK's rigid fist, then holds it wonderingly by the handle in front of himself, staring down at the blade. NICK snaps his fingers, crying –

NICK: Right! Carry on!

SOUND: *the droning stops.*
JOCK yells as his lunge ends with his lower

chest impaled on the knife. He falls down gasping
as the women jump up screaming. HONEY
rushes to kneel beside and wail over him.

HONEY: Don't die Jock! Don't die Jock! Don't die Jock!
O O O please don't die Jock!
JOCK dies. HONEY points to FLECK.

HONEY: You bloody murderer. *[weeps]*
FLECK drops the bloody knife, shaking his head
in a dazed way. The men stare at him, awestruck.
The women stare at JOCK's body. MAY puts
an anxious hand on FLECK's shoulder. NICK
smoothly addresses the company.

NICK: Ladies and gentlemen, you saw what occurred.
This poor misguided villain at my feet,
got drunk and, not knowing the great John Fleck,
tried to pick up his bird – his fiancée!
then tried to stab him, when John objected.
John, not wanting to harm him, moved very
fast to disarm him –

KODAK: By God he did!
I never saw a man move faster!

NICK: His martial skill saved **him** from disaster,
but alas, alack! – his attacker died
by committing accidental suicide.

HONEY: *[still sobbing]* O Jock! Jock! Jock!

NICK: What John Fleck did was done in self-defence.
Does anyone disagree?

SMELLIE: You're making sense.
KODAK, MACDUFF, SMELLIE and MARTHA nod
and murmur agreement.

NICK: We want no scandal in a club like this. *[he looks*
at MACDUFF]
What does our Procurator Fiscal say?
MACDUFF points a foot at the body.

MACDUFF: I know this thug. He's scum. Bad as they come.
Smellie, call the police. I'll talk to them.
SMELLIE leaves.

NICK: Since we all agree, I'll talk to the press
and ensure there's no publicity for this mess.
HONEY springs up, screaming at NICK.

HONEY: You killed him! You made my Jock drunk
and led him on! **Why** did you? **Why**?
*With clawing fingers HONEY tries to attack
NICK, is held back by TOADY. NICK shrugs,
extending his arms to the company.*

NICK: To that question I have no reply.

KODAK: The poor kid's hysterical.
*HONEY embraces TOADY, weeping on his
shoulder. WAITER hands TOADY, who is
weeping too, a glass of whisky which he
holds to her mouth muttering –*

TOADY: Drink this Honey. It'll do you good, really it will.

MAY: Please take me home John! I feel ill.

FLECK: *[rousing from his stupor]*
Sorry dear. We must wait for the police.
*He sits down gloomily with his arm round
MAY, who clings to him. The rest sit down
except LEE who stands, approaches FLECK
and bows to him.*

— ACT 3 —
THE MEDIA

The blue drop curtain covers the back central door. On
the left, a platform with hanging cameras pointed at it.
This platform later serves as TV studio but at first serves
as a church porch from which steps descend to an
open touring limousine. Round the car stand chatting
press, radio and television reporters, photographers
and cameramen. On the right, a table and five or six
chairs are first a street café, later a space for a studio
audience.

SOUND: *The triumphant conclusion of Mendelssohn's Wedding March.*

FLECK and MAY, dressed as a newly married couple, with NICK as best man, appear on the platform. FLECK and MAY pause to be photographed while NICK descends steps and opens the car's back door. They follow him down, climb in and sit back. NICK closes the door and stands near as the journalists swarm round them.

KAY: Mrs Fleck, how do you feel after wedding Global Boss's most highly paid consultant?

MAY: Wonderfully happy.

PEE: How, John, does it feel to **be** Global Boss's highest paid consultant?

FLECK: It's a responsibility.

CUE: What will they consult you on?

FLECK: Everything.

PEE: War on terror?

CUE: Global warming?

KAY: Your favourite reality TV star?

PEE: Do you oppose stringing up paedophiles by the balls? If not, why not?

CUE: What about economic textual process and its internet nexus nascent commodification?

KAY: Posh Spice? Heather Mills?

NICK, smiling but firm, intervenes.

NICK: Ladies and gents, please! A little moderation! This is John's wedding day.

FLECK: What I have to say will be said when I have had time to give these urgent questions due consideration.

PEE: But your sex tips for newlyweds?

FLECK stares at him.

NICK: *[smoothly]* John's not that sort of celebrity.

KAY: Mrs Fleck, what's **your** advice to newlyweds?

MAY: Tell the truth, I suppose.

NICK: And never never never get found out!
General laughter.

PEE: You're his spin doctor?
NICK gets into the driver's seat saying –

NICK: Certainly not. No,
John writes his own speeches. I just move and
mind him. Let's cheer John and May off on their
honeymoon! – Hip hip!

THE PRESS: Hooray!

NICK: Hip hip!

THE PRESS: Hooray!

NICK: Hip hip!

THE PRESS: Hooray!

*FLECK stands up, raises hand for attention. A
silence in which NICK changes his top hat for a
chauffeur's cap.*

FLECK: I must say one thing. Science can devise
cures for all the worst threats to our planet
that we communally recognise.

CUE: You have hope for the world?

FLECK: We must not despair.
NICK starts the car saying –

NICK: On that good note, goodbye to the lucky pair!
*Amid cheers FLECK, MAY, NICK drive away.
Everyone else settles down at the café as WAITER
serves drinks. The three reporters are at the table,
PEE dejected, CUE calmly cheerful, KAY repairing
her make-up.*

CUE: What's wrong?

PEE: I'm short of nouns. I envy you.

CUE: Why?

PEE: The Guardian lets you use nouns with more
syllables than one. I've just two words for rotters –
beast and fiend.

CUE: You could say rat.

PEE: We do!
Love rat ain't bad, but rat is too mild for
terrorists, paedophiles.

CUE: Louse?

PEE: Too small.

CUE: Sod? Turd? Shit? Poo?

PEE: No fucking use.
In the tabloids bad language is taboo.
I hate this job sometimes.
*KAY pauses in applying make-up and points
to PEE saying –*

KAY: Gloating in gore and gruesome gabble,
you're a paltry pimp who panders to the rabble.

PEE: *[nodding]* Too true.

CUE: What do you think of Fleck?

PEE: Another mouthpiece, hired to make excuses
for all the Global Boss's worst abuses.
[scornfully]
"Science can devise cures for all threats to
the world that we recognise!" – like Hell it can!

CUE: That could be his aim. He thinks like Einstein.
He's new to the media game.

PEE: Don't talk rot.
They pay him to be a parrot – a tame parrot
like me.

CUE: I don't see that.

PEE: Course not! You disagree
because you're an owl. You shut your eyes
to what our bosses don't want us to advertise.

CUE: That's partly true. *[sighs]*
      A wise old owl lived in an oak.
PEE: The more he heard, the less he spoke.
CUE: The less he spoke, the more he heard –
PEE & CUE: Let's emulate that wise old bird!
      They chuckle, pleased with themselves. KAY, feeling left out, says –
KAY: Cuckoo!
      PEE and CUE stare at her.
KAY: Cuckoo! Cuckoo! Cuckoo!
      KAY points at PEE and CUE saying –
KAY: If **you** are a parrot and **you** are an owl,
      I'm a cuckoo making a cheery noise
      to help women readers think it's always spring –
      All three start singing –
CUE: When birds do sing hey ding-a-ding-a-ding –
PEE: – hey ding-a-ding-a-ding –
KAY: – hey ding-a-ding-a-ding –
KAY, PEE & CUE: Sweet lov-ers love the spring!
      This has drawn attention from the rest of the media team. All stand and sing –
CHORUS: Parrots, owls and cuckoos!
      Happy folk are we.
      We have not much to tell you but
      we talk talk talk talk talk talk talk talk about it –
PEE: Squawk about it!
CHORUS: Till you finally agree.
PEE: Parrots, owls and cuckoos!
      We speak and talk for you.
KAY: Our platitudes are endless but
CHORUS: we tell them tell them tell them tell them tell
                them tell them –
KAY: We do we do we do!
CUE: Till you come to think they're true.

CHORUS: Parrots, owls and cuckoos!
    KAY: And also many geese!
    PEE: And if you say we're shameless
                         ruthless greedy selfish liars –
    CUE: That's libel!
    KAY: That's libel!
    CUE: That's libel!
    PEE: So send for the police.
CHORUS: Yes, send for the police!
            Send for the police!
            Send for the police!
            Send for the police!
            Everybody leaves, CUE going last and telling the audience as he departs –
    CUE: The police, of course, are a last resort. We're usually sufficiently compensated through civil actions in a law court.
            CURTAIN at back rises to reveal the terrace end of a Californian mansion, with beside it a lawn backed by beautiful flowers under a sunny blue sky. FLECK and MAY sit on each side of a table with the parasol casting shade over them. FLECK wears white trousers, shirt, unbuttoned waistcoat and silver untied necktie, with a white jacket on the back of the chair behind him. With two typed pages on the table beside his machine, he is busily typing a third. MAY, in a loose gown, contentedly breastfeeds their newborn baby. NICK, wearing flame-patterned Bermuda shorts sunbathes nearby with a Sex-On-The-Beach cocktail at his side, completely relaxed but listening to every word spoken. MAY raises her head, looks lovingly at FLECK and asks –

MAY: How did we get all this?
     FLECK pulls the page from his machine saying –
FLECK: Global Bosses think I'm worth it.
MAY: You are!
FLECK: Not me. But in a day or two, perhaps,
     I just might be.
     FLECK glumly looks through the typed pages.
FLECK: Some bosses will think me very bad, May
MAY: *[slightly worried]* Not all of them?
FLECK: Hard to say.
NICK: Hooray!
     By the pricking of my thumbs,
     horrid mischief this way comes!
     NICK jumps up as FLECK stands, dons jacket,
     lifts pages, goes to MAY, bends to kiss her.
FLECK: You and the wee one have nothing to fear.
     You'll both be alright.
MAY: *[alarmed]* Does that mean **you** won't be?
FLECK: Don't fear for me, dear. I'm leaving on business,
     but Nick will keep me safe – won't you Nick?
NICK: *[saluting him]* Sure boss! Sure!
FLECK: So there's no need for distress.
     MAY, reassured, attends to baby. FLECK leads
     NICK to centre stage.
FLECK: You love mischief?
NICK: *[nodding]* Only mischief makes me laugh.
     FLECK hands him the typed pages.
FLECK: Show Global Bosses this speech I will make
     to the United Nations on their behalf.
     NICK looks quickly through them, muttering –
NICK: Third world nations' corrupt officials are
     to blame for deaths and contamination.
     Employers Federation will prevent
     a repetition of the accident.

Hum, how does it end? Waste of life and land
will end, economic growth maintained by
measures introduced without reckless haste ...
NICK becomes indignant.

NICK: This bland stuff **mischief**? A gross mistake!
This is dull ordinary mischief unless ...
Is this really the speech you're going to make?

FLECK: Listen and see.

NICK: By G! ... Ahem! By economic growth,
John Fleck you start to fascinate me.

FLECK: I've never asked you for anything, Nick.

NICK: *[nodding and grinning]*   True!
All you ever wanted just **came** to you –
love, riches, a child, fame –
You! Just! Somehow! Got!

FLECK: I ask something now.

NICK: *[eagerly]*   Indeed? What? What?

FLECK: My speech tomorrow
may lead to public disgrace.

NICK: Wonderful!

FLECK: Get May and baby into a safe place
before that. It is the one thing I ask.

NICK: *[airily]* With my connexions that is a simple task.
*FLECK lays a hand on NICK's shoulder saying
sternly –*

FLECK: Make May and our child safe. This you **must** do!
NICK sighs and rolls his eyes upward saying –

NICK: Human sentiment! I loathe it but **shall**
see to it. Anything to oblige a pal.

FLECK: Thanks! *[hesitates]* Can I do something for you?
NICK is greatly but secretly amused.

NICK: No no no.
Just be yourself. All that **I** want will follow.
NICK walks back across the terrace and out,

ignored by MAY contentedly nursing baby.
CURTAIN descends, shutting off the terrace.
A big television screen is lowered before the
CURTAIN. It shows Westminster Palace viewed
across the Thames.
Simultaneously, a large screen with a similar
view is seen on left platform behind a table
with carafe of water and glasses. TV PRESENTER
appears there too and stands looking down at
FLECK who, in a leisurely way knots his necktie,
buttons his waistcoat, produces comb from
inner pocket and tidies his hair. KODAK and
LEE enter right and shake hands with FLECK.
NICK, wearing black jeans, scarlet sweater, also
enters, hands LEE the typed speech, slaps FLECK
encouragingly on back. FLECK turns and climbs
stairs to the platform, shakes hands with the
PRESENTER and sits with him chatting amicably
at the table. LEE, KODAK and NICK sit at the
table on the right, LEE nodding approvingly
over FLECK's supposed speech. NICK relaxes
ostentatiously, one leg over the other and hands
clasped behind head. They are joined by PEE,
CUE and KAY who sit down to observe the
broadcast, obviously expecting to be bored.

SOUND: *da-da-da introductory music for news*
broadcast.
The PRESENTER's head appears on the screen as
he speaks from platform.

PRESENTER: For deaths and contamination caused
by meltdown in Taiwan, the Green Party
claim that nuclear industry is to blame.
Global Employers' Federation have
commissioned an investigation by

an impartial scientist, prize-winning
John Fleck. He will speak to you in their name.
*FLECK's head appears on screen as he
speaks from platform.*

FLECK: This disaster killed a quarter million folk
and poisoned half a nation. Some say it
is the nation's fault, and the Federation
of Global Bosses won't let it happen again.
This is a lie. I will explain why.
*KODAK, horrorstruck, stares at LEE who
frowns thoughtfully. PEE, CUE and KAY sit
up, startled and pay close attention. NICK
cuddles himself, grinning.*

FLECK: This event, as all scientists know,
is in a series begun many years ago
before Three Mile Island and Chernobyl
made it plain. To stop worse happening again,
worldwide co-operation **must**
replace competitive exploitation.
*KODAK, writhing, tears at his hair. PEE, CUE
and KAY express consternation and delight.
LEE crumples up the typescript in his hand,
impassively glancing at NICK who covers
face with hands, to hide that he is enjoying
himself.*

FLECK: Exploiting folk, like too much booze, makes some
feel great but ends in the collapse of those
who win, as well as those who lose, but if
we equally share the good things we make,
none need despair. We can now use the sun
as a power station giving us free
abundant harmless energy **without**
fossil fuel and atomic radiation!
Yes! We can now end poverty and build

a truly democratic civilisation
without dictatorship! One-party states
go bad, as we saw in Russia, but now
a worldwide money market dictates
laws to every nation through the richest
and most warlike nations, especially
Britain, China and the United States.

*LEE gives KODAK rapid instructions. KODAK
leaves as LEE takes out mobile phone and dials.
The PRESENTER takes out his mobile phone,
listens attentively.*

FLECK: I call on employers everywhere **not**
to amass wealth. Please use it to create
freedom from want and fear and to prevent
all our children's children dying in chains
of hideous accident —

*LEE and PRESENTER pocket their phones and
the PRESENTER's face replaces FLECK's on the
big screen as he says –*

PRESENTER: I must interrupt!
A terrorist bomb threat is making us
leave the studio at once! Now! Pronto!
John Fleck will end his speech when security
says it is safe to do so. We will show
meanwhile *King Kong Versus Godzilla.*

*On the big screen King Kong Versus Godzilla
begins. The PRESENTER and FLECK stand.*

FLECK: Is that true?

PRESENTER: Yes, that's *King Kong Versus Godzilla.*

*Exit the PRESENTER. FLECK, after a thoughtful
pause, descends slowly to the stage as LEE tells
NICK –*

LEE: You lied when you said we could trust him!

NICK: *[shrugging]* He fooled me too.

LEE: You know what we must do?

NICK: Of course! I'm sure it will work like a charm
if you're fast enough.

LEE: *[grimly]* We're fast enough
to stop him doing colossal harm.
*Exit LEE. NICK joyfully meets FLECK centre
stage.*

NICK: John Fleck, congratulations!
You've put a real tiger cat among the
pigeons, parrots, owls, cuckoos, bats, rats, moles,
and also hedgehogs of the United Nations.

FLECK: I told the truth.

NICK: And now want to see May?

FLECK: Of course.

NICK: O you poor souls! You told the truth
but forgot a big fact.

FLECK: What do you mean?
*NICK waves a didactic forefinger saying
pompously –*

NICK: Woman is an anchor of the flesh
Restraining honest men's accomplishments
What did Kipling say?
"Down to Gehenna or up to the Throne,
he travels the fastest who travels alone."
A pity about your wife and wee one.
FLECK recognises something appalling.

FLECK: But you've put them in a safe place!

NICK: *[with sadistic relish]*
As safe as our Global Bosses want it to be.
*FLECK punches his own brow with both
fists, screaming –*

FLECK: You lying bastard!

NICK: *[amused]* That comes as a surprise?
I am Nick! The Foul Fiend! Prince of Darkness!

Lord of the Flies! Do you seriously expect
Satan **not** to tell lies?
KODAK enters briskly.

KODAK: Leave him to me now Nick.
*NICK sits down at table to the right and finds
what follows very entertaining.*

KODAK: OK, Fleck. Want to hear from your wife and child?

FLECK: Yes! Yes!

KODAK: *[looking upward]* Give him sound.

SOUND: *MAY is heard sobbing, a baby screaming. Later
her voice is heard.*

FLECK: *[aghast]*   What is happening to them?

KODAK: Listen for a while and she'll tell you herself.

MAY'S V.: Help! Can **nobody** hear me?
O baby don't cry like that…

FLECK: *[yells]* Stop it! Stop whatever you're doing to them!

KODAK: Have a word with her. *[hands FLECK mobile phone]*

FLECK: May, can you hear me? Can you hear me May?

MAY'S V.: O John, where are you John?

FLECK: Where are **you**?

MAY'S V.: I don't know, it's so dark here,
perhaps I've gone blind?
O please baby don't cry like that!

FLECK: *[begging]*   Please, please give her light!

KODAK: Alright. *[looks upward saying]* Give her light there.

MAY'S V.: *[sharp scream]*

FLECK: *[frantic]* What's happened dear?

MAY'S V.: A light went on.

FLECK: What do you see?

MAY'S V.: Everything's white … and cushiony …
I'm on the soft floor of … a padded cell,
I suppose … with a big television screen …
[wildly]
It's showing horrible things! Horrible horrible things!

[she weeps]
FLECK: *[yelling]* Turn that set off!
KODAK: I'll do better. *[looks upward]*
                          Change the channel.
MAY'S V.: *[screams then laughs hysterically]*
FLECK: What's **happened**? What's **happened**?
MAY'S V.: They're showing *The Simpsons!*
KODAK: *[looking upward]*   That'll do now.
SOUND: *is cut.*
KODAK: When shortly we agree, tell her from me
       all will be fine. You will see her tonight,
       after you broadcast the end of your speech
       and make everything right.
       KODAK takes mobile phone from FLECK,
       gives him a typed page.
KODAK: This is how it ends.
       Make no mistake! You will say it well
       to save your wife and child from a living hell.
       For their sake, look at this picture.
       KODAK holds out a photograph. FLECK,
       after a glance, claps his hands and the paper
       over his eyes. KODAK says inexorably –
KODAK: Look again! You may find it hard to believe
       that the woman and child in it are alive.
       Strange what modern medicine can achieve.
FLECK: *[wildly]* You are evil. Obscene.
       KODAK shrugs.
KODAK: I disagree, though I know what you mean.
       I have a family and love it too,
       which is why I am persuading you
       to say what we want. Now read that!
       FLECK stares at the page, asking hoarsely –
FLECK: Must I unsay the truths I told?
KODAK: You can't!

Millions were enthralled by what you said.
Those words cannot be recalled. Now you'll say
global businesses and governments will
do what you want when some years of delay
gives them time to get changes underway
and save the world for everyone.

FLECK: Will it?

KODAK: Eventually.

FLECK: That **cannot** happen if you delay!

KODAK: You must sound as if it can, or –
*KODAK again thrusts photograph before FLECK
who writhes, moans –*

FLECK: I've no choice.

KODAK: None. None. None.
*KODAK pockets photograph, his voice becoming
friendly –*

KODAK: And now, John Fleck, rejoice!
Good news. The Bosses are all **still** your pals.
Play ball with us! You, your wife and child can
live secure in a good place while the rest
of the world turns into manure.
FLECK giggles hysterically.

FLECK: Secure?
Where? On the moon? Or a nuclear bunker
where we stew until stifled by our own
unrecyclable shit?

KODAK: No no no. The bunker option is for
politicians who paid for it, and will
die there, like you say. You, your child and May
can share clean air and luxuries on an
island scrubbed from maps and prepared when we
saw we'd made mistakes that can't be repaired.
There you, John Fleck, great scientist, can help
the world's owners plan a better world while

wars, famine, plagues wipe clean the nations
rotten with overpopulation. You,
May, your child, can die with them in pain and
be forgotten with that scum! Or live well
with we who will rebuild the world anew!
Which do you choose John Fleck? Heaven or Hell?
FLECK writhes, watched keenly by NICK who
has risen to his feet.

FLECK: We'll … go with you.

KODAK: You have chosen well.
NICK, clasping hands above head and
shaking them triumphantly, rushes to KODAK
and pats his back in congratulation.

KODAK: Come, Nick! We'll let John prepare his broadcast
[he points to the paper FLECK holds]
These words will be on teleprompt but first
learn to pronounce them trippingly on the tongue,
but not too fast.
KODAK and NICK leave. FLECK crouches on
floor, right hand holding the speech clutching
the other elbow, left hand clutching brow.
He rocks to and fro, muttering –

FLECK: O God God. O God God. O God God.
GOD, looking like nobody special, approaches
and squats by him, smiling slightly.

GOD: You are worried, Mr Fleck.
FLECK ignores him.

GOD: *[sighing]*   You are worried. Yes.
FLECK, in agony, still hardly notices him.

FLECK: I'm nothing. Nothing. I can do nothing.

GOD: You're wrong.

FLECK: Eh?

GOD: You can give it all up.

FLECK: What do you mean?

GOD: Say goodbye to the lot.
FLECK: My wife? My child? O no. O no.
GOD: *[cheerfully]*   Leave them!
FLECK: Help other folk by putting them in hell?
GOD: No. Leave the others as well.
FLECK: Truth? Honesty?
GOD: Keep those. Leave the rest.
         FLECK stares, realises something, slowly nods.
FLECK: That would be best. But how?
GOD: Feel your pocket.
         FLECK feels in his side pocket.
GOD: No. Inside.
         *FLECK feels breast pocket, finds something, pats
         it, then smiles as if seeing GOD for first time.*
FLECK: I know you now! Thanks! You are –
         GOD places a finger on FLECK's lips
GOD: Don't say!
         GOD leaves. NICK hurries in.
NICK: Who was that?
FLECK: I thought you knew everyone.
NICK: In busy times some faces I forget.
         Well, John, have you learned your speech yet?
FLECK: Promise me something now that you **must** do
         since even greater mischief will ensue.
NICK: Your wish is granted before you ask!
         You! Really! Are! A **tremendous** toff!
FLECK: Before my speech ends, let nobody cut it off.
NICK: You'll damn May and your kid to a living death?
FLECK: No.
NICK: If you obey Global Bosses, who **can** cut you off?
         *FLECK grabs him by the shoulders and
         violently shakes him saying –*
FLECK: Do what I say! Let all folk hear and see
         me everywhere for three minutes! Three! Three!

Three minutes! Promise me! Promise me!
NICK, enjoying this, giggles girlishly until
FLECK, disgusted, releases him.

NICK: He he he! He he he! He he he he!
[*pulls himself together*]   Amazing!
I've been manhandled only once before,
in the Sinae desert, year nineteen Anus Domini.
Adorable John Fleck! How you **rrrrravish** me!

FLECK: Give three minutes or...

NICK: What?
After a pause FLECK suddenly grins and says –

FLECK: I kill myself.

NICK: Eh?

FLECK: I will kill myself.
NICK is serious for the only time in the play.

NICK: I don't want that.

FLECK: But that would win your bet with God!

NICK: Not quite.
It would be a nil-nil draw, no fun for me.
[*thoughtfully*]
Three minutes! Hm. You could, you just might beg
Vox Populi to make all things right, but
[*suddenly cheerful*]
that will do no good! Three minutes I guarantee.

FLECK: See to it Nick.
FLECK turns away, adjusts clothing, then
slowly climbs stairs.

NICK: [*thoughtfully*]   He's up to some trick.
What can it be? Surely he can't outsmart **me**?
LEE and KODAK enter right. NICK joins them
and talks to them genially. They sit at the
table as PEE, CUE and KAY occupy other
chairs. FLECK, on platform, sits at table with
PRESENTER.

SOUND: *Da-da-da   introductory   music   for   news
           broadcast.*
           *PRESENTER's face appears on screen at back as
           the group to the right sit up watching closely.*
PRESENTER: Today a terrorist bomb threat cut short
           John Fleck's talk on his investigation
           into the Taiwan meltdown on behalf
           of the Global Bosses' Federation.
           It is now safe for him to continue.
           John Fleck, over to you.
           *FLECK tears in two and flings away the paper
           speech.*
FLECK: The start of my speech frightened those who don't
           want to make this a good world for each man,
           woman, child – those who think monetary greed
           alone drives folk to make what we need,
           but true wealth is **not** in stocks and shares
           traded and stored in banks by billionaires
           enriched by high prices and warfare –
           *The following happens during the rest of FLECK's
           speech. Consternation in the studio audience.
           LEE takes out his mobile phone, dials, finds it
           does not work, dials again without result, flings
           it onto table, speaks to KODAK who hands him
           his mobile phone. LEE dials and finds it too does
           not work. PEE, CUE and KAY make the same
           discovery with their mobiles. The PRESENTER,
           disturbed by FLECK's speech, takes out his own
           phone, dials a higher authority for instruction,
           finds it does not work. He sees the studio
           audience have turned their attentions to NICK
           who they think responsible because he finds
           their confusion amusing. With vehement shakes
           of the head, spread hands and shrugs he signals*

bewildered innocence. The PRESENTER descends to the floor and joins this group. Baffled, all turn and stare at FLECK on the platform or screen.

FLECK: Poverty and wars will only end when true governments agree. The only true governments are and must be the people! You! People must not wait for politicians to improve their state. Your parliaments should be where you meet in farm, shop, school, factory, office, garage, hospital, police station, street **and** church! **And** regiment! Let it be **you** who decide what your nations do. Make, move and sell nothing you know is bad or made by folk who are badly paid. General strikes will force reform. Above all, do not kill! Choose no leader who can or will tell you to kill. Ban killing! Those who won't obey you when you ban that, will certainly betray you. *FLECK stands, spreading arms sideways in an appeal that for a moment gives him a crucified look.*

FLECK: Surely even the rich can now see that exploiting people just to make money is a horrible, destructive way to be!

NICK: Dear me, he **is** intense!

KODAK: Millions of fools will think he's talking sense! *FLECK, still standing, leans forward, hands on the table, gathering strength for his final words. KODAK shouts at the PRESENTER –*

KODAK: Cut him off ! Why can't you cut him off quick?

PRESENTER: Every channel of sound is jammed –

KODAK: – except that damned TV!

LEE: Explain that Nick!

NICK pulls mouth down at corners, shrugging.

NICK: I suppose the anarchist underground
is being helped by Marxist boffins in the BBC.

FLECK: Lastly, to my wife who is watching me
while held hostage by Global Employers,
I have this to say. Don't be afraid. They
won't hurt you now. I love you. Goodbye May.
*Pulls small pistol from inner breast pocket, shoots
himself in head, falls forward on table. Everyone
seated jumps to their feet. NICK screams –*

NICK: No! No! No! No! No! No! No! No! No! No!
No! No! No! No! No!
*NICK leaps from stage and runs out through
audience howling no! no! no! until silenced by
distance.*

SOUND: *The distant low noise of a disturbed crowd. This
grows louder till the play ends, but so gradually
that at first none on stage need talk louder to be
heard above it.*
*LEE, KODAK, PRESENTER, PEE, CUE, KAY rush
up onto platform. LEE and KODAK carry off
FLECK's body. The rest sit at the table and the
face of each appears on the screen as they
speak, starting when NICK's last no! is made
inaudible by distance.*

PRESENTER: Yes. Today Professor Fleck, Nobel Prize winner,
had a nervous breakdown on worldwide news.
He committed suicide after making
wild allegations while speaking on behalf
of the Global Employers' Federation.

CUE: Though a great scientist, the extra strain
of investigating Global mishaps
clearly drove John Fleck insane.

KAY: How could he bear to shock his wife and child

in that dreadful way? Every woman alive
must sympathise with May.
*MAY appears on screen with the baby in
her arms, staring wildly ahead at an invisible
teleprompter.*

MAY: **Nobody** held me hostage! **Nobody**
threatened to hurt baby and me. Global
people have been very good to us! Now!
Now especially! Poor John **must** have gone mad!
[a sob]
He was not a bad man! John loved baby and me –
cared for everyone –
he was always kind and good, never bad! *[weeps]*
O he **must** have gone mad!

PEE: But evidence
received by the Procurator Fiscal
proves that John Fleck stabbed to death
a young drug dealer in a night-club brawl.

SOUND: *The crowd noise has increased. Distant
voices grow audible among it.*

VOICES: Fleck told the truth! The truth! Fleck was right!
[etcetera]
*From now on the speakers' faces no longer
appear on the telescreen which shows jostling
crowds holding placards and banners saying
"FLECK WAS RIGHT" in several languages.
The speakers now need to raise their voices
above crowd noise.*

PRESENTER: A former colleague of Fleck claims that he
funded visits to Thailand child-brothels
by selling drugs to students at university.

CUE: Fleck, demanding peace and preaching class war
just did not know what civilisation is **for**!

PEE: Paedo Fiend Fleck Exposed At Last!

This perv had the nerve to incite revolution,
while corrupting students in a public institution
and abusing kids abroad! Young kids! **Young** kids!
He should have been hung!
*The demonstrators on screen are violently
attacked by police and/or troops using tear-gas
and water-cannon.*
FRENCH, GERMAN, RUSSIAN VOICES CRY –
Il a dit la vérité! Er hat die Wahrheit gesagt! On
skazal pravdoo!
*CUE, unhappily influenced by international
protest, shouts –*

CUE: Let us heed just this: Fleck's indication
that the Federation's corporate greed
endangers every nation, did not wholly mislead…

PEE: What the hell does that mean?
On screen tanks are rolling toward crowds.

SOUND: *Uproar is now so great that CUE and PEE are
only just heard yelling –*

CUE: He told the truth!

PEE: Single syllables eh? Okay!
*PEE picks up a megaphone from under the
table and bawls into it –*

PEE: Fleck was right!
Noble Nobel Boffin Blasts Global Boss Beasts!
Workers of the world unite!

SOUND: *Blast of gunfire.*

LIGHTS: *All lights cut except on screen where the tanks
open fire.*

SOUND: *Huge explosion.*
*The screen goes blinding white then red then
fades into total darkness.*

EPILOGUE AT
HEAVEN'S GATE

SOUND: *Grandly solemn chords of religious music as in Prologue, while stage back drop curtain slowly rises upon:*

LIGHT: *Backdrop of dawn sky with rising sun as in Prologue.*
THE THREE ANGELS stand as in Prologue and chant this slightly shorter hymn –

RAPHAEL: The sun star, glorious as ever,
                    bathes all his worlds in golden light,
          still rolling round the galaxy
                    midst nebulae as vast and bright.

GABRIEL: Swift, unimaginably swift
                    the mighty earth is rolling too,
          from darkness of profoundest night,
                    to skies celestially blue.

The voice of NICK is heard as he staggers drunkenly through the audience, shouting loudly over the angels' voices, until he mounts the stage.

MICHAEL	NICK
While winds contest with ocean waves	Fuck you all!
or drive them on like fleeing crowds	Fuck you all!
against the base of granite cliffs	Fuck you all!
whose summits penetrate the clouds –	Fuck you all!

GABRIEL	NICK
Storm clouds, whose snow & hail & rains	Fuck you all!
in stream and cataract pour down	Fuck you all!
to flood and irrigate the plains	Fuck you all!
ensuring growth is nature's crown –	Fuck you all!

RAPHAEL	NICK
That seeds take root and creatures feed	Fuck you all!
from humble worm to beast of prey	Fuck you all!
while angels, heralding The Lord	Fuck you all!
announce the dawning of His day!	Fuck you all!

> *NICK collapses on stage hammering it with his fists and groaning as the angels chant –*

ALL THREE: While sounding colour glows and leaps
                    twixt star and sun and world and moon
            God is the harmony that keeps
                    all nature's orchestra in tune!

LIGHT: *GOD's spotlight shines on NICK.*

GOD: You are drunk, my friend. Sorry you lost our bet?
NICK: I can't go on!
GOD: *[kindly]*   Poor Devil, you want peace
         only possible if life would finally cease.
NICK: Let it cease! Why not? Why stop me making
         everything die? Everyone should!
GOD: They always do.
NICK: Why must you keep creating them anew?
         I loathe the screams of women giving birth.
GOD: I suffer with them. With them I recover.
         The universe requires me for her lover,
         don't you know?
NICK: Yes! Since you both cast me out
         millions of years ago!
         NICK rises to his knees, weeping.
GOD: You left because you hated us, Old Nick.
NICK: Because I foresaw your foul arithmetic,

that multiplies the swarms of life on earth
with germs of every size, constantly giving birth.
Life is a foul disease that I must cure!
I beg you, please! Please! Please!
let's sterilize the world and make it pure!

GOD: Love will not let me – love that drove John Fleck.
NICK leaps up yelling –

NICK: To suicide?

GOD: He gave folk hope that greed
will not destroy the planet they all need
to share and live upon in liberty –

NICK: *[yelling]*   Equality? Fraternity?
Cretin! Can you not see, won't you confess
the fight for these prolongs the human mess?

GOD: Fleck did not want the human race to end
and you, poor drunkard, only feel distress
because you came to feel he was your friend.

NICK: *[weeping]* My only friend!

GOD: *[laughing]* Apart, of course, from God!

NICK: You shit! You squirt of piss! You stinking sod!
You **Nobodaddy**, nastier than worms
infesting earth because you love their squirms!
GOD addresses his angels.

GOD: My better children, come back to the sky
and there enjoy the better things we do.
Make life the loveliest form of energy
that every day creates the world anew.

SOUND: *A grand Amen.*
NICK pulls himself together.

NICK: God fucks off as usual into air –
thin air – leaving the stage to me and my
despair. Hm. Am I desperate? Not quite!
Fleck's speech has spread confusion.
Prompted by me, chaos, war will ensue.

If nuclear fires burn the planet black
life may **still** turn back to eternal night!
NICK addresses the audience enthusiastically.

NICK: Adieu, kind friends, adieu, we'll meet again
through famine, poverty, disease and pain!
I hope our entertainment pleased you well
— it has no moral. See you all in hell!

AUTHOR'S POSTSCRIPT

AS A CHILD I WAS A GLUTTON FOR STORIES OF magic and miracles so came to know all the fairytales pantomimes are based on, besides the talking animals and animated toys of Kenneth Graham and A.A. Milne. The Bible was not among the books in our home – faith in education was my parents' only religion – but at school my religious instruction was mostly Bible readings, so I came to know many tales about fiction's oldest, most famous and most influential character, God the Dad.

He fascinated me because (unlike his son Jesus Christ who was probably real) God's dealings with people were horribly unfair. He makes the first man and woman ignorant of right and wrong, but gives them easy access to knowledge of right and wrong in a fruit they are commanded not to taste. He has also given the garden a clever serpent (why?) who prompts them to eat it, which they do, for they can only know it is wrong to disobey God after doing so. For this crime they and their children are punished by lives of hard labour ever after. This single-parent God is obviously a twister, but a convincing twister, who contrives for his children what Ronald Laing calls a double bind: the situation of being wrong because they exist. Like other early gods the Ancient of Genesis liked the smell of burnt food. Adam and Eve's son Cain tilled the soil so could only offer vegetables, so God preferred his brother Abel, a shepherd who roasted mutton for him. We are not told how God showed his preference, but it made Cain so jealous that he murdered Abel. It is good that God did not retaliate by killing Cain, but marked him so that others would know he was a public danger. Much later God tells the children of Israel "Thou shalt not kill" then tells them to invade Palestine and massacre the natives.

I now know my teachers steered clear of several Biblical stories showing God at his worst, but am still surprised by how his believers justify these. The Reverend C. H. Mackintosh, in an 1879 introduction to *Deuteronomy*, wrote, "some persons, allowing themselves to be influenced by morbid feeling and false sentimentality … find difficulty in the directions given to Israel in reference to the Canaanites. It seems to them inconsistent with a Benevolent Being to command His people to smite their fellow creatures and show them no mercy. They cannot understand how a merciful God could command His people to slay women and children with the edge of the sword." Mackintosh then explains that folk who cannot understand this are presuming to judge God, when they should have the faith to know that everything He commanded in the Bible was right. In 1941, sixty-two years later, *The Bible Today*, published by Oxford University Press, had a commentary excusing the massacre of Ammonites, Midianites, Canaanites and Philistines because the Israelite invasion was a "life-and-death struggle between truth and falsehood for the cultural development of God's people." In 1941 the Nazis were planning to promote German cultural development by killing every Jew in Europe. My only excuse for the Old Testament God is that he caused everything, so is the father of everyone but especially Jesus, whose Sermon on the Mount should have wholly replaced the Ten Commandments. But Christian, Muslim and Zionist governments have preferred the Old Testament Dad whose words justified invading, killing and robbing those who thought differently from them, and many who thought almost the same.

But I could not dismiss Nobodaddy (Blake called Him that) as a fantasy like the Wizard of Oz. If God was the soul of the universe like I was the soul of my body, then newspapers and history books showed that innocent, helpless people *were* still being hurt and killed on a universal scale, so the soul of the universe often **IS** horribly unjust. This sensible assumption would not let me rest and gave me an appetite for stories about how evil happens.

Six centuries before Christ was born, Lao Tze wrote that the cause of all things is not nameable, but those who need a name should call it Mother. Alas, my education made it impossible for me to think the soul of all things was female. I also wanted to name the not-nameable in a way that made me think it *essentially* good. My earthly dad, Alex Gray, did not need to do that – he thought God a name for something he did not know, so need neither accept nor reject. Like many others he had lost the Christian faith of his parents when fighting in France, so had directly experienced more evil between 1914 and

18 than I have met in a life of 73 years. He seldom spoke of his war experiences, thought evil sprang from human greed and ignorance, and that wars and exploitation would end in the victory of co-operative Socialism, though the struggle for this might last centuries. He was enviably content with this faith. The struggle he believed in had achieved many good things I enjoyed – our comfortable council house, my schooling, the public libraries, the National Health Service – but the victory over Fascism that founded the British Welfare State in 1945 was soured by the needless testing of the first atomic bombs on two big Japanese cities, after which the biggest nations invested huge wealth in a nuclear weapons race that was supposed to save the world from Communism, and is now supposed to save it from terrorism but is really maintained because the arms industry is Britain and the USA's most profitable source of investment, and gives them means of bullying poorer nations. Needing to believe in a creative goodness more lasting than people I searched for it through literature and art, and found much in the works of Bernard Shaw and William Blake who, surprisingly, sent me back to the Bible.

Both of them pointed out that, even before Jesus arrived, it contained more than a blood-thirsty battle god hell-bent on destruction. He is found speaking like the demon of Socrates, not in thunder but in a still, small voice. He threatens to punish an evil empire with worse evil, but spares the wrongdoers when they repent and beg for mercy. Prophets arise who, speaking for God, denounce sacrifices – say the smell of burnt offerings stink in His nostrils, because the rich Jews are using these to win His favour while exploiting their poorer brethren. He promises that if they obey Him and love their neighbours as themselves, everyone will adopt their faith and wars will cease because (as Burns puts it) "Man to man the wide world o'er / Shall brothers be for all that". Blake especially pointed me to *Job*, the Bible's eighteenth and most humane book.

It is a unique poem which does *not* ascribe evil to human disobedience and folly, but to The Lord (as God is named here) who starts by calling a conference of his heavenly sons. One of these is Satan, who is allowed to patrol the earth and spy on it, like a secret service chief reporting to a prime minister. The Lord (rather smugly) says Satan can have found nothing wrong with Job, a perfect and upright man who not only obeys God's commandments, but sacrifices burnt offerings on behalf of his seven sons, in case one of them has secretly sinned by cursing God in his heart. Satan replies with a question, "Is Job not highly paid for trusting you? He is spectacularly rich. Remove his possessions and see what he thinks of you then." God refuses to do that but lets Satan do it. Job's seven sons and three daughters are killed by lightning and a storm knocking their house down, while invading foreigners kill all his servants and steal his thousands of camels, oxen, asses and other worldly goods. Job, now a childless pauper, says, "I was born naked and will die naked. The Lord gave and the Lord takes away. Bless Him!"

So at the next heavenly conference the Lord can

still boast of Job's faith. Satan points out that, despite Job's losses, he still has his health. So Satan is allowed to make Job's skin erupt in such dreadful boils from the soles of his feet to the top of his head that soft ashes are the only seat he can bear. He squats in them, scraping his scabs with a piece of broken pot. When his horrified wife tells him to curse God and die he answers, "Shall we receive good from God and not receive evil?" Worse evil comes to him in the form of three old friends who try to persuade him the evils he suffers are God's punishments for sins he *must* have committed – by claiming he has never sinned he casts doubt on God's justice, so deserves to suffer. At this restatement of the bad old parental double-bind The Lord intervenes on His own *and* Job's behalf, telling the friends they don't know what they are talking about. In a great hymn to the glory of the universe He declares that it is too vast for human minds to completely understand, so people must accept the universe and the Lord who made it. What else can they do? Beyond this point *The Book of Job* ends unconvincingly with Job being finally given more wealth and children than he originally lost. *Job* is the only Old Testament book where Satan appears. He appears just once again in the Bible when tempting Christ in the Wilderness. These are the Devil's only Biblical appearances. *Genesis* does not suggest that Satan was the snake who tempted Eve and Adam.

After the crucifixion Satan's power was hugely magnified by a revolutionary Christian doctrine claiming that God gave a new immortal soul to every *body* at birth. Greek Pythagoras, Indian Buddha also

thought souls were immortal, but had been created
with the universe, after which everyone who died was
reborn in a different body. Most religions, including the
Jewish, thought death ended the soul, though one or
two great folk might be carried up bodily into heaven
and live there eternally. Most funeral rites were to
ensure the dead *stayed* dead, and did not trouble the
living as miserable ghosts. Egyptians assumed the soul
disintegrated with the body, so those who could afford
it tried keeping bodies *and* souls together by having
their corpses mummified and securely entombed.
An early pharaoh sought immortality by having his
mummy stored with many of his riches in the world's
heaviest tomb. Raiders were too smart for him. A few
centuries later an Egyptian scribe lamented that even
the builder of the Great Pyramid was now, like the
poorest slave, dust blown around the desert sands.
So when Christianity declared everyone was equally
immortal, whether slave or emperor, it spread fast
through the Roman Empire whose basic activity was
slave-making.

But immortality was a threat as well as a glad
promise, since only *good* Christians would enter
heaven after death. Fathers of the Christian church
decided that, since Adam and Eve's disobedience,
Satan was the God of this world because all natural
forces and nearly all people were ruled by Satan,
who was no longer a son of heaven allowed by God
to walk the earth as His secret policeman, but a fiery
rebel whose main kingdom was Hell – the lowest
part of the universe in the world's centre – with the
surface Hell's suburb where new-born souls graduated

to heaven or hell after death. Nearly every earthly pleasure, especially sexual pleasure, was denounced by the church as a Satanic snare. Christians still exist who think that way. When that assumption was more widespread it is not surprising that the Devil became popular, especially after Roman Emperors made Christianity official. For about sixteen centuries after that there were tug-of-wars for supremacy between Christian churches and Christian governments, but usually they got on well together, so critics of either were condemned as Devilish. The clergy found Satan indispensable. Description of Hell's tortures were the strongest part of many sermons. Thomas Aquinas, theologian and Saint, declared that viewing the agonies of the damned were half the delight of Heaven. The logic of Aquinas became the limit of Roman Catholic philosophy for centuries. Those who tried to know more were often condemned as heretics.

The story of Faust became widely known shortly after the invention of printing. The name of an early German printer was attached to the wicked hero of a puppet play as famous as the story of Punch, and very similar. Faust pawns his soul to enjoy twenty years of unlimited knowledge, wealth and mischief before the Devil collects it. Kit Marlowe, Shakespeare's great forerunner, was a homosexual atheist and a member of the Elizabethan secret service which finally murdered him because he knew too many state secrets. He was also a popular playwright whose *Doctor Faustus* emphasises the knowledge that gives Faustus invisibility, air-flight and time travel. But

Marlowe's Devil, Mephistopheles, after one or two fine speeches, becomes a mere prankster – not an interesting character. Apart from his two Old and New Testament appearances the Prince of Darkness made no great appearance in world literature before Protestant Milton took him up. In Dante's *Inferno* he cannot even move, being a three-headed giant frozen upside down in the world's dead centre.

For centuries Milton's *Paradise Lost* was accepted as England's greatest poem and Satan is certainly its greatest and most sympathetic character. Being enthusiasts for the French Revolution, William Blake and Robert Burns greatly admired this archetypal rebel. Blake pointed out that after creating the universe Milton's God does nothing but forbid and punish, so all creative energy is left to Satan and his followers. In the 20th century *Paradise Lost* was disparaged by Ezra Pound and T.S. Eliot, who thought it made better sound than sense. The critic Leavis found Milton's supernatural universe full of contradictions, also pantomime slapstick in the Heavenly war between angels and devils who try hard but cannot seriously injure each other. But the contradictions in *Paradise Lost* are all in the Bible and what Christians have since made of it, and Milton has deliberately compounded them by adding every other convincing vision of the universe offered by Greek legend, New World geography and Renaissance science. Milton probably believed what God told Job's false comforters – that understanding Him is too big a job for the human brain, but he felt it right to try, and would probably have defended the contradictions in *Paradise Lost* as

Walt Whitman defended those in *Leaves of Grass*: "Do
I contradict myself? Very well, I contradict myself. I am
vast. I contain multitudes." Before the 20th century
most Believers accepted the contradictions. Voltaire
mocked them because he was a sceptic for whom
God and the nature of the universe were identical.

Then at the height of European Enlightenment in
the late 18th century, Goethe arrived and gave the
Devil a new lease of post-Christian life.

A 20th century German author (perhaps Spengler?)
wrote that modern man lived in a Faustian age
where human powers had been hugely increased by
Devilish bargains. It is a fact that literary masterpieces
from Goethe's *Faust* onward are about wealth and
power gained or sought through evil – Stendhal's
Red and Black, Wagner's *Ring*, Dostoevsky's *Crime
and Punishment*, Dickens' *Great Expectations*, Ibsen's
plays. Strangest of all, bestsellers about supernatural
evil were written by folk without faith in the
supernatural – *Frankenstein*, *Dr Jekyll and Mr Hyde*,
Trilby, *Dracula*, *A Picture of Dorian Gray*, *The Wild
Ass's Skin*. The last is Balzac's only supernatural tale.
His realistic ones indicate that criminal bargains are
well worth striking if you are smart enough to keep
the gains. Thomas Mann's novel *Dr Faustus* describes
a great German composer born soon after Bismark
unifies his nation, who deals with the Devil shortly
before World War One, writes masterpieces, but
finally goes insane when Hitler comes to power.

I was fourteen in 1949 when the BBC Third
Programme celebrated the bicentenary of Goethe's
birth in a fortnight of broadcasts about the man and

his work. For several nights it broadcast the five acts of *Faust*, and its vast scope so excited me that I bought a Penguin translation of *Parts 1 and 2* by Philip Wayne, and acquired Victorian translations of the whole by Bayard Taylor and John Anster. I easily enjoyed inconsistencies as bad as any in *Paradise Lost*. Like *The Book of Job*, this play starts with God allowing the Devil to test the faith of a good old professor whose knowledge of life is theoretical. Mephistopheles restores Faust's youth, helps him to seduce a young and loving girl, kill her brother in a duel, then abandon her when pregnant. Maddened by shame and loneliness she kills her baby and dies in jail, refusing Faust's last-minute efforts to free her because she fears his devilish friend. It is a richer play than that bare outline, mixing supernatural events with the social variety and humour of a Dickens novel, but written in poetry only those who know German appreciate. Yet the inferior English verse translations excited and delighted me.

Goethe was a young man when he wrote this first part and a famous middle-aged German writer when it was published, staged and acclaimed. Coleridge considered translating it, Delacroix illustrated it, Berlioz and Gounod set it to music. Goethe's admirers thought that if he completed *Faust* it would be to Germany what the *Iliad* had been to Greece, the *Aeneid* to Rome, the *Divine Comedy* to Italy – a display of Germany's cultural greatness through the power of her language. In 1832 at the age of eighty-three Goethe published the end of the play and died a few months after.

With the Devil's support Faust is now shown creating modern commerce by inventing paper money, saves Europe from civil warfare by hiring a mercenary army, time-travels to Ancient Greece, learns much ancient wisdom and returns with Helen of Troy. Their son has some of Lord Byron's traits, but Faust does not need family life. He acquires land by forcibly evicting peasants, imagines he is building a great new home for mankind by reclaiming desolate seashores, and becomes too old and blind to know or care that Mephisto has financed all his grand schemes by theft and piracy. After death he is conducted upward through angelic circles dimly recalling Dante's *Paradiso*, and left reunited with the pure spirit of the first woman he betrayed. What more could any man get? We all have fantasies of absolute power and absolute approval. No wonder the slightly miserable youth I was in 1949 liked that play.

Nietzsche thought the play's weakness was a German professor needing Satan's help to seduce a woman of the servant class. I disagree. The weakness is its unstinting sympathy for a billionaire businessman always enriching and aggrandising himself while claiming to seek the highest good. In the play's earlier part Faust briefly regrets harming Gretchen but neither before or after does he regret using Satan to get all he wants. He dies at his smuggest. Goethe, using the literary device of Faust's immortal soul, might at least have put him through a purgatory that taught him the harm he had done. No. Satan tries to seize the soul he has earned by so much hard work, and the angels cheat him out of it because (they say) "He who

unwearedly kept trying, we have the power to free."
– an excuse for Julius Caesar, Ghengis Khan, William
the Conqueror, Napoleon, Mussolini, Hitler and Stalin
who could all have said with perfect honesty, "To the
end of my days I never had a moment's rest." God
in Heaven starts Faust's adventure, but even Goethe
flinched from showing Him at the end, telling His
angels to cheat the Devil.

What finally makes Goethe's *Faust* structurally
inferior to the epics of Dante and Milton is its almost
total indifference to Christianity. In the first act Faust
is restrained from committing suicide by a cathedral
choir celebrating Easter morning, which reminds him
of his innocent youth. Thereafter Jesus has no place
in his world-view, because the mature Goethe was as
much a pagan as any ancient Greek or Roman.

So Goethe's Faust joined God the Dad as fictions
haunting me because both represented powers
abroad in the world that I could not be at peace with.
Over the years God excited my imagination (which
Blake said was the Holy Ghost in people) to write
verses about Him with more and more sympathy.
Nobody imagining God can help making Him in their
own image, so of course He became for me an artist
struggling with difficult materials, some of them in his
own personality. I have never been able to take Satan
seriously – he is all too human – but in 1999 I saw
Glasgow Citizens Theatre perform Marlowe's *Doctor
Faustus* in a version by Edwin Morgan. This kept all
the great poetry, replacing the slapstick clowning
with modern devices – the infernal contract signed
in blood became a mainline drug injection, the

three books of infernal knowledge were compressed into a laptop computer. This so impressed me that I suggested to Eddie that he should now write a more satisfactory version of Goethe's *Faust*. He found the idea unattractive. Perhaps like Hugh MacDiarmid he disliked Olympian Goethe for turning Faust into a successful businessman who goes to heaven.

In 2006 I wrote *Goodbye Jimmy* for the Glasgow Òran Mór lunch hour theatre, a play whose main character is an absentee God who is finally shown subordinate to the Great Mother of All Things. Perhaps that prompted my own attempt to translate Goethe's *Faust*. The Prologue and First Act were completed by Hogmanay 2007 and those who know Goethe will see it only contains what he invented, though I have compressed much and omitted more. Not knowing how to continue I sent it to a Director of the Scottish National Theatre, hoping for a commission to research it further. The script was returned because the Edinburgh Lyceum had recently performed another modern version by John Clifford, so I decided to change Faust's name to Fleck and make him a Scot. At the time I was working hard on a book I had been busy with for years and had promised to give the publisher at the end of April 2008. Halfway through April I faced the fact that my *Life in Pictures* book could not be finished so soon, told my publisher I would finish it in a year or two, and enjoyed a wonderful freedom that suddenly let me finish *Fleck* in four or five weeks, helped by Helen Lloyd and Roger Glass who had been my secretaries while working on other books.

I am happy to have completed this play with a Faust/Fleck who, though not a Christian, becomes briefly Christ-like and beats the Devil, helped by a God who ends the play besides starting it, while briefly interfering with the plot. Nick is identical with Goethe's Mephistopheles but no other characters are, except perhaps God. Goethe called his *Faust* a tragedy, which his ending stops it being. I call *Fleck: A Comedy* because dying well is the happiest thing anyone can do if they don't believe in personal immortality.

Alasdair Gray, 29th August 2008

GOD POEMS
1955-2005

CRIES FROM UNCEILINGED BLOOD

1
In the beginning was the cavity,
eye-socket in no skull, wound in no flesh,
the faceless mouth, the coatless pocket.

This got such horror of its own vacuity,
it tried at length to scream, as who would not?

Then, after aeons fighting voicelessness,
it screamed a nebula of hydrogen.

Odd that the Jews should so have misconstrued
that scream a word, that cavity a God.

2
Then life appeared, a cancer of the clay:
some molecules chance shuffled into sense
that wriggled out into the light of day:
a knot of fibre twitching in the firmament
with no provision for its government.

CRIES FROM UNCEILINGED BLOOD

3
Mind is a sky machine
kept stable by the breeze of breath,
a rackety slipshod thing of gut and nerve,
patched tube and twisted cable.
The engines of the heart and lung sustain
its wings above the basement of a void.
Boxed in its skull, brain is the aneroid
                         by which we gain
a level through the pressure of our pain,
struggling hard for some
degree of stable equilibrium.

4
Corruption is the Roman whore for whom
hangmen and politicians play the pimp.
She sucks all semen back into her womb
and issues from the pastures of the thighs
bastards who momently repopulate
the oceans, rocks and skies.
The coffin is no more
than bawdy house for that grand Roman whore.

CRIES FROM UNCEILINGED BLOOD

5
Just as the sun
  is one spark
    in a tremendous dark

so love is a point of heat in all that cold
  felt by the young and very old who know
    all footprints must be blotted out with snow

and out of love we sit
  with hunger gnawing at our wit
    and ears cocked for the bark
      of mouthing anarchy crouched
                beastwise in the dark

alone alone cold cold cold and alone
  inside the black vast
    eternally revolving
      remorseless engine of the whole.

6
God is a bleak fact in a book of stones,
a cold voice in a room of iron clocks,
a frozen hoof that clatters on my bones.

CRIES FROM UNCEILINGED BLOOD

7
These factors (pain and death) are
                                essential factors,
geared to the earth's ellipse and
                                motions of the belly.
Enclosed by a void, enclosing an abyss,
I by detesting such essential factors
have set the void to war with the abyss
                                and tear me harder.
I will not be torn.

  Still an implacable voice shrieks in the sun,
  these insults strike at the face of the sun –
  oppose them!

O do not doubt I know my danger.
Movement requires friction, blood is
                                struck in the heart,
every awareness implies some sort of collision,
but to fight pain and death with every weapon
will make war total, leave no hope of peace.
I will have peace.

  Still an implacable voice shrieks in the sun,
  these insults strike at the face of the sun –
  oppose them!

CRIES FROM UNCEILINGED BLOOD

Is it not right to attempt to be like God?
To gain an equal acceptance of larks and cancer
and to go gentle into that goodnight?
Yes, total acceptance is death
                              for something human
but accepted death is seldom troubled by pain.
I have been man too long.

> *Still an implacable voice shrieks in the sun,*
> *these insults strike at the face of the sun –*
> *oppose them!*

98

CRIES FROM UNCEILINGED BLOOD

8
Who unpick their anatomy
in ecstasy and agony
can find their self within no part
of backbone, belly, brain or heart.
Selfhood is the unity.

I tried to know a deity
who justified morality
and found a good god cannot fit
the outer void, the inner pit.
God is the iron grid of law
                    upholding the totality.

9
Or else the brightness without edge
                    informing the totality.

from *Old Negatives*, Jonathan Cape 1989.

ADAM AND EVE

Perhaps because I planted it too far north
the park today is showing signs of dearth.

It is not good for man to be alone
but did I give the keeper's wife so sharp a tongue?

Why do they now sit brooding, back to back?
What does she find so charming in the snake?

It will drive the other beasts wild,
                         but naming them
(the keeper knows) is a way of taming them.

So why use jagged tools to manage my zoo?
And break bits off my tree?
                 GET OUT! BOTH OF YOU!

written for woodcut in Ian McCulloch's
The Artist in His World, Argyll Publishing, 1989

POSTMODERNISM

In the beginning was the Word,
and the Word was with God,
and the Word was God.
God said, "Let there be light."
All things were made by him.
In him was life;
and the life was the light of men.
And the light shone in darkness,
and the darkness partly understood
and lectured on it.

Light died before the uncreating Word.

Now darkness lectures to darkness upon darkness,
and the darkness sees that it is good.

from *Sixteen Occasional Poems,*
Morag McAlpine, 2000

GENESIS

Light dawns without commanding.
Sense precedes understanding.
Crying, crooning make language,
say what gets believed.
God who sees all creation good
is to be achieved.

from *Sixteen Occasional Poems,*
Morag McAlpine, 2000

GOD AGAIN

I brooded on dark water
       though neither fish nor bird,
an unembodied voice
       who made all things by word,

made light, sky, sea and land,
       creatures that glow and grow,
bodies that shine above
       and root, glide, creep below.

Seeing all this was good
       I wanted people who
might share my admiration
       of everything I do.

Though always bodiless
       I have a certain form
so modelled it in clay,
       gave breath to make it warm.

You are my image folks,
       greater than all you see
in intellectual scope,
       but not as great as me.

Your dreadful faults, alas,
        reflect what I desired:
a lust to make new lives,
        a lust to be admired.

New lives made with labour,
        bodies requiring breath,
come to displace their makers,
        condemning them to death.

I will not mend the faults
        that generate your woes.
Mistakes can be creative too,
        as every artist knows.

first published in *Stand* magazine, 2005

GOODBYE

www.tworavenspress.com